SAANJH

vermillion symphony of the day's adieu

SAANJH

vermillion symphony of the day's adieu

JC Swayamshree Mohanty

BLACK EAGLE BOOKS
Dublin, USA | Bhubaneswar, India

Black Eagle Books
USA address:
7464 Wisdom Lane
Dublin, OH 43016

India address:
E/312, Trident Galaxy, Kalinga Nagar,
Bhubaneswar-751003, Odisha, India

E-mail: info@blackeaglebooks.org
Website: www.blackeaglebooks.org

First International Edition Published by
Black Eagle Books, 2024

SAANJH
by **JC Swayamshree Mohanty**

Copyright © JC Swayamshree Mohanty

All rights reserved. No part of this publication may be reproduced, stored in a retrieval system, or transmitted, in any form or by any means, electronic, mechanical, photocopying, recording or otherwise without the prior permission of the publisher.

Cover & Interior Design: Ezy's Publication

ISBN- 978-1-64560-635-2 (Paperback)

Printed in the United States of America

carrying a mind full of chaos, and a heart full of deafening silence

नीलाद्रौ शंखमध्ये शतदलकमले रत्नसिंहासनस्थं
सर्वालंकारयुक्तं नवघन रुचिरं संयुतं चाग्रजेन।
भद्राया वामभागे रथचरणयुतं ब्रह्मरुद्रेन्द्रवंद्यं
वेदानां सारमीशं सुजनपरिवृतं ब्रह्मदारुं स्मरामि ।।

"Saanjh- Vermillion Symphony of the Day's Adieu" is a celebration of emotions, intricately woven into words that echo in the nuances of time and memory long after they are felt. The author's voice carries a depth that transcendas her years, weaving vulnerability and strength into evocative verses.

May this poetic journey mark the beginning of a luminous legacy. In 'Saanjh' lies a soul unbound, resonant, and eternal.

Dr. Sujata Sahu
Principal-Cum-RO
DAV Public School, Chandrasekharpur

Mentor's Note

"Saanjh ~ Vermillion Symphony of the Day's Adieu" is a symphony of emotions, raw and resonant, woven with exquisite artistry. It is rare to witness a young mind articulate such profound depth, blending vulnerability with strength, and fragility with resilience.

To my student, the author—your words are a mirror to the soul, a bridge to the unspoken. May this debut be the first of many milestones, each more luminous than the last.

To the readers—immerse yourself in this tapestry of thought and feeling. You are in the presence of a voice that promises to linger.

With pride and blessings,
Mr Mayukh Mishra

JC Swayamshree is a girl whose intelligence sparkled in every room she entered, a bright light amidst the ordinary. Her curiosity knew no bounds; she asked questions that many dared not, challenging the status quo and seeking deeper truths. Her mind, a labyrinth of ideas and thoughts, constantly works to find connections that others missed. She has an innate ability to make complex concepts seem simple, as though the world is a puzzle she is always eager to solve. Her brilliance is not just academic; it transcended textbooks and lectures. She sees beauty in the patterns of nature and in human behavior. Conversations with her were like stepping into a world of innovation. She listens intently, her observations sharp and perceptive, often revealing insights that others can never notice. Despite her intellect, she remains humble. She never seeks attention nor admiration, though her brilliance naturally draws it. Her passion for learning is contagious. Whenever she speaks about a subject she loved, her enthusiasm is brightly visible. She faced challenges head-on, not with arrogance, but with quiet confidence. Her intelligence gave her the strength to overcome obstacles that would have defeated others. She never gave up, always finding new ways to approach a problem until it was solved. There were times when she was frustrated, but she saw failure as a stepping stone, not a setback. She is kind, compassionate, and thoughtful. She believed in the goodness of people and worked to bring out the best in them. Her presence commands attention, not by force but through the quiet strength of her insights. She has a way of making others see the world through a different lens. Whether in a debate or a casual conversation, JC's words are thoughtful, measured, and impactful. Her journey is one of continuous growth. JC's story is one of embracing change, seeking improvement, and staying true to her values. With each step, she inspires those around her to be better, to think more critically, and to always aim for greatness. I wish her all the best for "Saanjh"

Mr Sanjaya Kumar Satpathy

●

Dear JC Swayamshree, I am overjoyed to see your dream come into life. Your extraordinary voice, unique perspective, and creative craft have woven together into a collection that is both deeply personal and universally relatable. Your poetry is a testament to your creativity, vulnerability, and dedication to your art. You have showcased the most complex themes and emotions with sensitivity, uniqueness, and skill. As you put forth your work infront of the world, remember that your words have the power to touch hearts, spark conversations, and inspire others. Your poetry book is not just a collection of verses – it's a gift to your readers. I am honored to have been a part of your writing journey. Keep nurturing your creativity, staying true to your voice, and sharing your talents with the world. Congratulations on this remarkable achievement! I look forward to seeing the impact your poetry will make.

Mrs Amrita Trupti

•

A young writer, JC has attempted to convey the basic human feelings and emotions in the 7 Stages of Love. The book is touching, and filled with understanding as it traces the development of love and its various forms and stages, which is quite impressive, considering her age. JC's talent for describing such multi-layered feelings is astonishing. Her collective work is indeed an artistry never imagined before. Her writing brings to reality, the various aspects of life and relationships. This is an excellent achievement, there is a lot more success waiting for her and it's an excellent beginning of her literary career.

Dr. Lipsa Mishra

•

It's my pleasure to know that JC Swayamshree is going to publish her book. I always bless her with great success in life. May she prosper a lot in future!

Mr Sanjay Kumar Sahoo

Acknowledgement

First of all – akdlsfjskjdieasskkk *internally screaming*

Second, I can't believe this is happening. I would always be grateful to my teacher, Sir Mayukh Mishra, for being a source of inspiration and encouragement for over the past two years. The majority of credits go solely to him. To all my friends, seniors and juniors - who have been a constant listener to my yaps, and have kept pushing me towards this, a whole hearted thanks to you and you better not boast reading this! To everyone who has commented or put up a shout-out for my words, I do owe you more than just an acknowledgement page. A greater piece of gratitude to my parents for the reverse psychology they used. And oh! How do I forget - Thanks to my muse for letting me write all these unaddressed letters.

Ajaa, I know you would have been the happiest person, if you were physically here.

Lastly, dearest Jaggu, I and Saanjh would have not been possible without you.

CONTENTS

ONE MOMENT I'M RESTING IN THE COCOON OF MY GLOOM, THE OTHER MOMENT YOU WALK INTO MY LIFE	19
WE DON'T LOVE EACH OTHER YET BUT I WOULD LIKE TO THINK WE DO	21
HAVOC	23
THE OCD OF LOVE	25
MY FORBIDDEN LOVE, IF TOMORROW DOESN'T SHOW UP FOR ME	27
AFTER YOU LEFT	29
73 SECONDS	31
HEART'S SHIFTS	33
DELETE. NO. BACKSPACE. DAMN. JUST SHUT DOWN	35
NOT YOUR TYPE	37
PLEASE UNDERSTAND MY NEED TO BE COLD	39
HIS EXQUISITE BLUES	41
WHAT STOPPED ME?	43
HOME	45
LET GO	47
YOU SHOULDN'T FALL IN LOVE WITH HER, FOR SHE	49
दिलकशी	५१
उन्स	५३
इश्क़	५५
अक़ीदत	५७
इबादत	५९
झूनून	६१
नौत	६३
BONUS - यादाश	६५
पांचाली	६७

If that doctor cuts open my heart, he'll fall in love too.

ONE MOMENT I'M RESTING IN THE COCOON OF MY GLOOM, THE OTHER MOMENT YOU WALK INTO MY LIFE

One moment you reach out to me with your shivering hands, the next moment I want not to let go of it so soon. One moment we talk about each other's preferences. The other moment we're on the list. One moment you ask for my permission to rest your head on my shoulders. The other moment I'm in your arms, looking up at the stars on the terrace of the *home* that we built. One moment you hand me a confession letter with *tiny flowers* drawn on it, the next moment you get on one knee to propose to me with a ring that has *our names engraved* on it. One moment you put your stethoscope on my chest, listening to my heartbeats, to make me realize how hard I love you. The other moment you sit beside my bed listening to our baby's heartbeats. One moment we discuss how our first pets left. The other moment we sit, deciding names for the new member. One moment I write notes for you as we don't get to talk every day. The next moment our first born giggles as he reads them as a bedtime story to the next one mentioning how crazy their mama loved you.
One moment, we're skeptical to tell each other *I love you*. The other moment we say *we do* to our happily ever after.

*A hopeless romantic falling in love is
Like a child unwrapping a chocolate
We exactly know what's in there,
But the heart gears up nonetheless.*

WE DON'T LOVE EACH OTHER YET BUT I WOULD LIKE TO THINK WE DO

I would like to call it love when I get back home to a bunch of messages saying *I was on your mind the entire day*. I would like to call it love when you randomly call me names just to catch a glance of the *crimson on my cheeks*. I would like to call it love as you confidently claim me as *your girl*. I would like to call it love for you to give me my robbed childhood back as you draw fishes for me. I would like to call it love as we spend our day discussing biology precisely about why your heart races *faster than Ferrari* as you see me. I would like to call it love when you overshare your details of the day. *I would like to call it love as I kiss your fisted hand out of the blue and you open it to show my name written on your palm.* I would like to call it love as you ask me to sing you to sleep and validate the voice which was hated by my entire bloodline. I would like to call it love as you purposely miss out on your close friend's b'day just to catch a few more hours with me before you leave for the other city. No wonder why they hate me. I would like to call it love as you made me learn, love wasn't about dying for each other but to make *every moment worth living for*.

Because the truth was never honest
And the dare is never daring enough

HAVOC

The last straw found me just before the broken cliff planned to give up on me and let my insides be caressed by the ocean beneath. Like every person who wanted to be found behind the *shroud* of wanting to be lost, I let the straw hold me. And hold it did. It held me with a might that the branches could never have. Just when I *birthed the hope* of being found again, the straw decided to let go of me. And amidst the peaceful chaos, my tense shoulders had already dropped as I found my home. No. Not the shore but the *tempestuous sea.* I belonged there. The roiling current *injected life into my corpse.* Each drop explored the craters of my being. I was absorbed by the devouring sea. It consumed me. One piece at a time. But is it even love, if I don't sing my demise into your ears, even in the *depths of abyss*?

Life is an irony.
A person with OCD falls in love with asymmetric things.
Like…like the asymmetric Himalayan valleys…like the human heart….like a desperate kiss…and like… like his amber eyes behind the myopic glasses.

THE OCD OF LOVE

I'm addicted to abandonment. OCD doesn't let my eyebrows un-crease until people, most likely the ones I love, leave. OCD makes me suck on abandonment as if it were a *pacifier* to a sound sleeping baby. Remember the times I used to run out of breath on your not-so-funny jokes? OCD can't help but remind me of those days when I try catching a breath during a panic attack. OCD is the compulsion to remember the sound of your heart and *rip off mine if it doesn't sync with yours*. OCD is hoping every scar on my body to be made by your *misaligned teeth*. OCD makes me a selfish lover not letting anyone lay their little finger on me because what if the germs seep in and infect the last ounce of love I have for you? OCD is the obsession to pat your head to sleep and pierce my nails into my skin after you've left. OCD is like plucking my veins and arteries to weave them into a comforter of promises and wait for you to tear it into shreds eventually. OCD turns me into an obsessive visionary as I get precognitive nightmares about how exactly you've *planned* to leave me.

Home is my lip trapped between your teeth.
(haven't been home since long)

MY FORBIDDEN LOVE, IF TOMORROW DOESN'T SHOW UP FOR ME,

Remember that I'd always (yes always) love you. Okay, safe side, let's say I'll always have a soft spot for you.
I hope someday, you wear that olive-coloured shirt and just because I said, the color suits you.
Remember that I love hearing about all your silly crushes. Doesn't matter if I don't wake up tomorrow, I want you to know that I'd still be waiting to listen to you whining about them.
You sound very happy in love. Remember that *I love seeing you in love.*
Someday, if you open my drawer, read all the poems that I didn't let you read. Remember that all I wrote was about or maybe, for you.
Remember that I'd be up at 3AM to *listen to your breathing pattern* over a call, just because you woke up after a nightmare.
Remember that, *forever was never enough time to love you.*
Even if there's no next sunrise for me, just know I used to listen to your playlist (yes the one we made together) every night and technically, that's the last thing I heard before I left.

So,
Look for me in a basket full of *strawberries*.
Look for me in the voice of someone singing our favorite song. I call it our favorite. Yours, because you actually love the song and mine because I hopelessly love you. I'm pretty sure that you don't know but I love red roses. Leave some at my grave. I'll act surprised.
Someday, if you don't find me anywhere, search for me exactly at the place you left me.

After you left, the ventilators beeped louder.

AFTER YOU LEFT

I come back to cold bed sheets, perfectly ironed and without a single wrinkle. My feet take me to the coffee table. I work and read until I pass out. *Sleep doesn't knock on my door these days.* The roses that you gave me are still fresh enough in the vase and so are my wounds. In this life of what has felt like a thousand years, I realize, *I have died a trillion times and lived only when you carried my corpse in your arms.* I see shadows in the rainbow and the jasmine bleeds. Oreo still demands the cookies you make for her and my kitchen is weirdly neat as we no more make weird dishes out of potatos. I kiss your photo umpteen times a day and look for a hand to hold as the lost child searches for a little finger in the crowd of predators. An abandoned child is never afraid of loss, they are only *afraid of the mirage* that love creates.

If you still have my right anklet, please don't return it.

73 SECONDS

You talk a lot. And when you fall asleep, you blabber more. This left no chance for the devil to enter my silent mind, *until that night*. That night when we sat beside each other. You suddenly went silent for *73 seconds*. Morons slowly seeped inside me. Now the mango juice has whitened, and there's depth under my eyes. Anklets don't ring in pairs anymore. The chocolate syrup on my glass table has almost bleached itself. The wind chime doesn't sound like "*I'm home*" anymore. It's summer and the roses have stopped blooming. Strawberries have dried in the basket. The henna on my hand has faded. The polaroids on my walls have started yellowing. That playlist has vanished from recents and doesn't play anymore. The laundry is still undone. No one turns off the tap. *I drown in my own colorless blood.*

"*That was brutal.*" I break the silence. "*No, it was peaceful*", you reply.

"In the beginning it'll hurt a bit"
-And then?
"And then, you feel nothing."

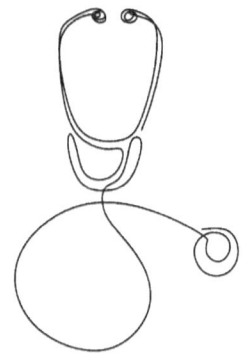

HEART'S SHIFTS

"You need to rest for-"
-"I hate doctors."
"Oh. Well. You must be hating me too."
"Umm no. Not you."

Under the dimmed OT lights, I chose to stitch the silence, more than my broken heart. Amidst the rhythm of these monstrous beeping machines, I blurt out - *"What's your genre in music?"*
-"Live heartbeats."
"So....You must be bored now. Aren't you?"
-"No. Why?"
"Because apparently my heart doesn't beat well enough?"
giggles
-You make everything so fun, Mama.
The rush of the staff's feet, the screams of the stretchers and the sirens of the ambulance made me slow dance into his "heart's shifts." Over the shared cups of caffeine, sleepless nights, stolen seconds of anguish and glances exchanged between the rounds and patient charts, he drew me in like the irresistible pull of the moon on the tide. The swab of alcohol crossed the barriers of my skin as the drips pushed me into a night of young romance. With each cut, he bore the excellence of fingers.
He was a doctor. Believed in miracles more than the obvious. His hands knitted me into what looked perfect to him. His blessed curse worked. White coat, round glasses and misaligned teeth became my destiny.

"You're a liar." He stated.
-"I don't —"
"Your heart beats the silent whispers of my favorite song."

*When the morning amnesia hits you, you don't really recognize the scars on your thighs.
So you prick it, to remind yourself of your very being.*

DELETE. NO. BACKSPACE. DAMN. JUST SHUT DOWN

That's how my brain feels. Just after waking up. I hate to wake up with a blank mind. The voices around me get louder and I lose my balance. Doctors call it *not-so-normal*. But you know right? I just need to think of something. Something that can put me into a loop. So I think. I think about what exactly I should think. Well- Oh! Maa making me a cute hairstyle. Oh! Baba carrying me around on the balcony. Oh! Nanna arranging my bookshelf. And oh him waking me up with a bed coffee. Him and Baba gently caressing my hair, whispering "Wake up, *Mama*. It's late." Oh no! Why do I see my maa shouting! Oh no! Baba ain't here to hold me and Nanna is no more. And Oh no. Oh God. I'm getting late and both Baba and him aren't pulling down the covers. But Oh! *I still hear their voices.*
Delete. Delete. Delete.
It's blurring out. I'm losing balance. Don't take me to the hospital. *That oxygen mask smells and suffocates.*

I close the door behind you.
So that no one else walks in.
Or maybe.
Because the door is too hard to open and
you stay for one more night.

NOT YOUR TYPE

You know, I'm no girl with sharp bangs and bright smile but I might pull the blanket over you and let your breath tickle *under the skin of my chest*. I'm no girl with slender fingers but I might make you a bed-coffee and serve you pancakes dipped in love and drizzled with honey. On a rainy afternoon, I'm no girl who plays an instrument but I might offer you my heart strings to play with or maybe make you paper boats - because mine were snatched.
I'm no girl who you could take on a *chai-coffee-jhumke* instagrammable date but I might make you a canopy out of my duppattas, the ones beaming with fairy lights and click a 1000 photos for you to post under your dead feed. I'm no girl with slightly tilted eyebrows and plump lips but I might kiss you like tomorrow is not guaranteed. You know, I'm no girl with a pretty round face who'd open the door with a wide warm smile, but I will leave the door open for you to come back.

*i-wish-you-didn't-ask-me
smile.*

PLEASE UNDERSTAND MY NEED TO BE COLD

Please understand my need to be cold. That's the only weather I've lived all my life.

It sucks to move past people like a ghost - something that's already dead but yet to be buried. How does it feel to be the *no-one-gives-a-fuck-if-I-leave* person?
It sucks to have a sinister satisfaction to miraculously string together the lives of others, especially when your own cries meet the cruelty of their blind eyes. How do you think it feels to be on the *number(especially the person behind)-is-out-of-your-reach* side of the call?

It sucks to have a pounding heart; it is a brutal reminder of my fragile existence. The last time my mother's words weren't daggers, when the ring of her anklets were not haunting and when her glass bangles didn't know how to pierce through my skin, has blurred out. How do you think it feels to be the *i-wish-you-were-a-still-born kid* live?

It sucks to have my father's shadow looming large in my dreams reminding me of the futility of my efforts. His love was the treasure I was always unworthy of. How do you think a *i-beg-you-to-not-introduce-me-as-a-father* child speaks about herself?

So dear *potential-next-trauma* , understand my need to be cold because I don't want to jolt up from sleep giving you a *i-know-you-would-leave-me-too* smile.

An art.

HIS EXQUISITE BLUES

His blues and greens swelled up as oceans on a full moon light. Fingertips glided over the veins - a canvas of desire, admiring the very essence of art. Throbs and pulses whispered the *unsaid intimacy - an invitation to dive deeper into depths of the young still night*. Under the dimmed moon light, storms built up as the oceans of love entwined with the whispers of shared secrets.

"you mean…forever?"

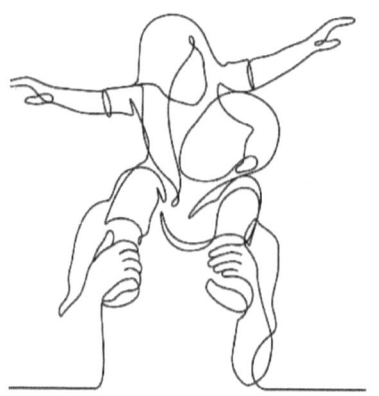

WHAT STOPPED ME?

Him. Mom. Dad.
"I still have to confess." I say to myself.
Deep down I know, I never will.
"She'll be waiting for me." I say to myself.
She's the one who said I'm a failure.
"He loves me the most". I say to myself.
But does he?
I think, "Isn't she able to see that her kid is burning in depression?"
"Can't he see, I've no energy left within, to keep going?"
Yet again, what stops me is-
"He'd need me when he's low."
"I was born outta her, would she be able to see me burning?
He heard my first cry, would he be able to carry down my dead body?"
"Am I being selfish? My life, isn't just mine.
After all, we don't live just for ourselves. Do we?"
The people who have pushed me into this, are the ones whom I live for
Crazy.

Home's a myth.

HOME

How hard is it to be 18 and walk into a home that has no broken hearts on the floor? A home where tears aren't the seasoning on every meal, where the tea doesn't spill on your hand and you don't have to stand in front of a splintered mirror? How hard is it to step into a space where laughter doesn't seem like a known stranger, the floors don't creak under the burden of angst? How hard is it to tip toe into a dim lit room without it swallowing you whole or to not find a flicker of the bed lamp and hold onto it as the last reason to live? How hard is it to stumble upon a bed that doesn't drown you or pump your lungs full with the weight of every cut?
How is it to be 18 and to believe the broken pieces of your heart could ever be swept out of under the rug and bandaged with love?

So hard or explicitly easy?

LET GO

You weren't lovers but you weren't friends either. For friends don't know, how your lips taste. They don't know how your body mist smells. Their heart doesn't seem to explode when you hug them. Friends, don't read books to you. Friends don't ask you to lay on their laps. They don't make you wear your shoes. They don't call you, half asleep, just to say that they missed you. But, life, more or less has to be in its form and now you end up reading your old chats to find comfort within them. You scroll down to find out the day when it all began, and now, you hate the fact that you cannot hate them. It actually gets messier with time. You check if they are online. You stay awake waiting for their text. And the worst part is, you can't even bid them a good bye, because basically you have no idea how to let them go. So you just end up waiting for them to drift apart.

Are you sure though?

YOU SHOULDN'T FALL IN LOVE WITH HER, FOR SHE

can't let go of things easily/ has miserable phobias/ would like to stick to you until you literally chop her heart off/ can't give equal efforts/ mostly dislikes physical contact. yeah, until it's you/ constantly wonders if someone is mad at her/ cigarettes don't kill her. family does/ cannot generally believe good things happening to her/ leaves the phone with the charger without turning the switch on/ out of 30 days on month, she's a sadist on 25 of them/ likes having maggi with ketchup/ dislikes both tea and coffee/ hates continuous rain/ doesn't generally explore music/ is just a step away from killing herself/ still waits for that one text/ pricks her skinout of anxiety/ misses him but wouldn't let him know/ waits for him to break the silence not her heart.

THE 7 STAGES OF LOVE

ये फ़ासले भी कम्भख्त कितने ख़ूबसूरत हैं।
हमारी शीश दिखाई में चांद आईना था।

दिलकशी

पहली नजर वाला इश्क - एक अनोखा फ़ितूर।
उस कंबख्त से नजरें क्या मिली, बादलों के पीछे से दिखने वाला चांद पूरी रात रोशन कर गया।
हवा का झोंका कुछ ऐसे आया की रूह को बेचैन कर गया।
उस कमबख्त से नजरें क्या मिली बिजली तो सीधे दिल पर उतर गई।
बारिश ने मोड कुछ ऐसा बदला की नजरें फिर से मिल गई।
अब ब्याग में पड़े काजल ने अपनी अहमियत जाता ली ,
और मेरी चिट्ठियों ने अपना पता ढूंढ लिया।
जवाब में गुलाब और इज़हार में झुमके मिले।
आईने का जिक्र फिर से होने लगा।

शाम की चाय अब कविताओं में बदलने लगी,
इश्क का फ़ितूर जो चढ़ने लगा !

उन्स

जबसे मिली हुं उससे एक खिडकी हमेशा खुली ही रखती हुं।
क्या पता कब ढूंढ़ ले वो मेरे सपनो की राह और पर्दों के पीछे से दस्तक दे जाए?
क्या पता कब चांदनी उसकी मुस्कान से शर्माए या सितारे अपनी नूर उसके होठों पे लुटा बैठे?
क्या पता कब रात की खामोशी उसकी धड़कनों से भरने लगे या हवाएं मेरे बिस्तर पे उसकी खुश्बू छोड़ जाएं?
क्या पता कब उसके हाथों का एहसास मेरी रूह को छू जाए या रात का अंधेरा उसकी आंखों की गहराइयां नापने बैठे?
क्या पता कब मेरे बालों की नमी उसकी उंगलियों में उलझ जाए और बांध ले हमारे दिलों को एक साथ?
क्या पता कब हम एक दूसरे में यूं खो जाए कि मेरी सारी हदें उसकी सांसों में घुल जाएं?
क्या पता कब वह पल आए, जब खिड़की के पार एक ऐसी दुनिया हो, जहां सिर्फ हम और हमारे जज़्बात के रंग हो।

इस खिड़की पे मेरे दिल का एक टुकड़ा है - जिसमें उम्मीद है, मोहब्बत है और इंतेज़ार की तो बैठक लगी है - शायद उसके दिल के किसी कोने में भी एक खिडकी खुली हो, जो मेरी यादों के इंतेज़ार में हमेशा महकती हो।

इसलिए जबसे मिली हुं उससे, एक खिडकी हमेशा खुली ही रखती हुं।

इश्क

अगर तुम मेरे हो ही नहीं तो पसंद आए ही क्यों ?
फूल को खुश्बू के सपने दिखाए ही क्यों ?
ज़रूरत थी क्या मेरी खामोशी को यूं आवाज देने की ?
तुम्हारे साथ जो खोए वो पल अब यादों में सजाए ही क्यों ?

जो बेकार था मेरा इंतेज़ार तो
मुझे रोका ही क्यों ?
नजरों से छूं कर जो तुम दूर चले गए
ये रिश्ता दिल का यूं बनाया ही क्यों ?

यूं ही गुजर जाता सफर तन्हाई का
फिर तुम बिन मौसम बरसात लाए ही क्यों ?
तुम जो मेरे ना हो सकते ये सच मुझसे छुपाया क्यों ?
उस झूठ में हमारे दिलों को यूं उलझाया ही क्यों ?
सपने अधूरे छोड़ने ही थे तो
मेरी रातों को संवारा ही क्यों ?
बिखरी हुई इन सांसों में अब तुम्हारी खालिश सी है।
पर इन्हें यूं सुलगती छोड़ गए .... आखिर आए ही क्यों ?

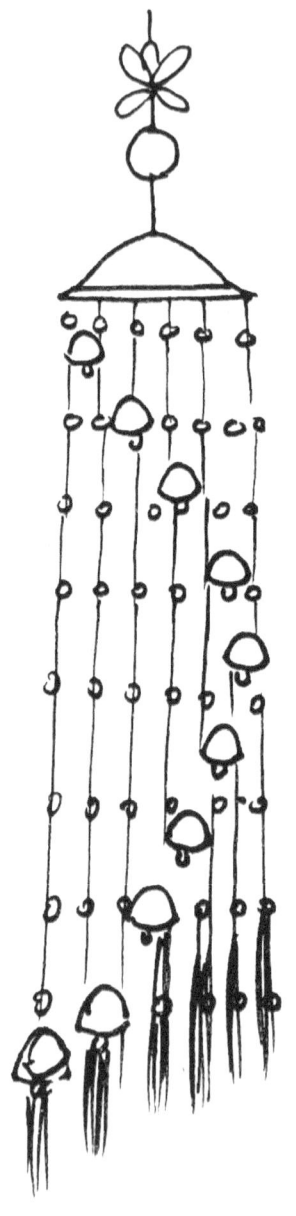

अक़ीदत

ना साथ है तेरा, ना कोई खबर
फिर भी दिल तेरा इंतेज़ार करता है बेखबर।
क्या तू जाने मेरी दुआओं में तेरा जिक्र है
हर शब तेरे ख्यालों का एक फिक्र है।
ना शिकवा है ना है शिकायत का शोर
यह इंतजार है मेरी अक़ीदत का नूर।

दूरियों ने तो बस दिल के रास्ते को महका दिया
जहां हम थे वहां खुद मोहब्बत का जादू था।

इबादत

कश्मीर जाना चाहती हूं।
आजतक नहीं गई क्योंकि लगता था, इतनी सुंदर जगह को अपनी आंखों में तो समेत हप्प पाऊंगी।

आज जाना है।
कश्मीर की गलियों में पश्मीने की खुश्बू और उत्तर की गर्मी ढूंढने।
नदियों की राह तकने और पर्दों के सिलवटों में सुकून ढूंढने।

आज जाना है।
दल किनारे कोई नज़्म लिखने और रबाब की कहानियों में इश्क ढूंढने।
नरगिस की महक और फिरोज की सिंदूर दानी में अपना घर ढूंढने।

आज जाना है।
वादियों की सुबह को देखने और किसी पहाड़ की छोटी पर अपनी आवाज ढूंढने।
कशीदे में लिपटे ख्वाबों को बुनने और शालिगंगा के पत्थरों में हमारे टुकड़े ढूंढने।

आज जाना है।
हर मंदिर में माथा टेकने, हर दरगाह में दुआ करने।
तुम्हारी चिड़ियों का पता और कश्मीर की बंध गलियों में,
तुम्हे ढूंढने।

जूनून

कैसे नाराज़ ना हूं?
मै तो खफ़ा हूं उस चांद से भी,
जिसकी रहनी ने तुम्हे छुआँ है।

मै पागल हूं शायद बेवजह ही सही
पर इस दीवानगी में भी एक अलग खुदाई है।
ये जूनून ही है जो रातों को जगाती है
ख्वाबों में इश्क के चादर बुनती है।

पर
काफी नहीं है क्या मुहब्बत मेरी,
जो तुम मिलते हो मुझे किसी और के सपनों में ?

मौत

क्या शायर क्या ग़ालिब मोहब्बत
उसकी एक झलक, दिल का सुकून मोहब्बत।
उसने दी जहर, तो तोहफ़ा मोहब्बत।
उसके मुस्कान सी खूबसूरत, मौत मोहब्बत।
कभी जज़्बात कभी सौदा मोहब्बत।
मर गए तो कहानी मोहब्बत।
जिंदा रह गए, तो मेरी जान ....

मोहब्बत।

BONUS - यादाश

जब मैं चली जाऊं, तो मुझे याद जरूर करना। तारीफ नहीं तो शिकायत करना।
बताना कैसे मै तुमसे पागलों की तरह प्यार करती थी।
कैसे तुम्हारे घर वापस ना आने तक, मुझे भी नींद नहीं आती थी।
कैसे तुम्हारे नाश्ता ना करने पर, तुम ही से झगड़ जाती थी।
बताना सबको की कैसे तुम्हारा मुझसे रूठना मुझे बेचैन करदेता था।
बताना सबको की मेरे बाद जो भी तुमसे प्यार करेगी, बेशक मेरी ही तरह तुम्हारे आंखों में खो जाया करेगी, तुम्हे दिन भर देखती रहना चाहेगी पर मेरी तरह तुम्हारी नजर नहीं उतारेगी।
बताना कि तुम्हारी जिस हंसी में मेरा प्यार बसता था, मेरा उस हंसी की वजह बनने का सपना मेरे साथ ही दफ्न होगया।
बताना सबको की दफ्न तो सिर्फ मै और मेरे सपने हुए हैं।
मेरे दिल ही हर धड़कन तो अभी तुम्हारे साथ ही है।

EPILOUGE

For the love of Krishn and the turmoil that *most* women go through-

पांचाली

कुरूराष्ट्र में बिछी थी सभा जगमगाई
आमंत्रित थे द्रुपद कन्या और पांच भाई।
शकुनि ने चली पहली चाल
सभा में छाने लगा अंधकार।
धर्म का रक्षण - क्षेत्रीय ज्ञान।
दाव पे लगाए अपने बाण।
पहले रखदी दौलत की बाज़ी।
फिर राष्ट्र, फिर स्वाभिमान और शस्त्रों पे संकट साजी।
आई कुलवधु के सम्मान पर आंच।
मौन रही सभा, किसी ने उठाई न आंख।

ये कैसा धर्म है जो आज चुप होगया ? पासों के खेल में सामग्री को तोला गया ?

कर्ण - जो पला था मा के कोख से दूर
कभी न समझ पाया नारी का गुरूर।
पत्नी बनकर जो रख न पाई लाज,
वह अब हो सभा में वस्त्रहीन। हो इसका उपहास !

खींचा दुशासन ने आंचल पांचाली का
वात्रहीन हुई सभा कौरवों की।

'गोविंद।'
गोविंद ने सखी का एहसान न भुला।

जो बंधन था द्रौपदी के करुणा का प्रमाण
कृष्ण ने दिया उसको दर्जा - रक्षा का वरदान।

जो जन्मी थी अग्नि से आज जल रही थी प्रतिशोध के क्रोध में।
फिर भी याज्ञसेनी ने अपना संयम न खोया।
आज अपमान हुआ है ये याद रहेगा।
मेरा विश्वाश कभी न मुरझाए, ये साद रहेगा।
जो रचाया आज अधर्म का राग
बनेगा रण भूमि के महाप्रलय का भाग।

कौरवों की हर बेइज्जती चुकाई जाएगी,
जब दुशासन के रक्त से पांचाली नहाएगी।

टूटेगी दुर्योधन की जंघा।
इसका संकेत लाएगी मेरे गांडीव की टंकार।

मेरा प्रण है तेरे स्वाभिमान का रक्षक,
मेरा प्रेम है तेरा धर्म, मेरा संकल्प शिक्षक।

राज्य, धन और भाई सब छोड़े थे कल,
पर नारी के अपमान का होगा अब पाताल तल।

पांडवों का ये वचन, एक प्रतिज्ञा है अमर -

जब जब पकड़ा जाएगा नारी का केश,
तब तब होगा महाभारत का युद्ध श्रेष्ठ।

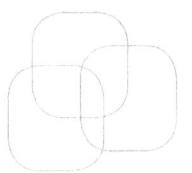

Black Eagle Books

www.blackeaglebooks.org
info@blackeaglebooks.org

Black Eagle Books, an independent publisher, was founded as a nonprofit organization in April, 2019. It is our mission to connect and engage the Indian diaspora and the world at large with the best of works of world literature published on a collaborative platform, with special emphasis on foregrounding Contemporary Classics and New Writing.

www.ingramcontent.com/pod-product-compliance
Lightning Source LLC
Chambersburg PA
CBHW030535080526
44585CB00014B/949